# Romantic Piano Anthology 1

30 Original Works
Selected and edited by Nils Franke

ED 12912
ISMN M-2201-2528-7
ISBN 978-1-902455-92-1

www.schott-music.com

Mainz • London • Madrid • New York • Paris • Prague • Tokyo • Toronto
© 2007 SCHOTT MUSIC Ltd, London • Printed in Germany

ED 12912

British Library Cataloguing-in-Publication Data.
A catalogue record for this book is available from the British Library
ISMN M-2201-2528-7
ISBN 978-1-902455-92-1

CD recorded in Champs Hill, West Sussex, 4th August 2007, on a Steinway D Concert Grand with Nils Franke, Piano
Producer: Ates Orga
Editor: Ken Blair

French translation: Michaëla Rubi
German translation: Ute Corleis
Music setting and page layout by Woodrow
Printed in Germany S&Co.8176

# Contents / Sommaire / Inhalt

## The Pieces / Les pieces / Die Stücke

| Title | Composer | Dates | |
|---|---|---|---|
| 1. Allegretto Grazioso | Cornelius Gurlitt | 1820-1901 | 17 |
| 2. Mélodie | Félix Le Couppey | 1811-1887 | 17 |
| 3. Song without Words | Fritz Spindler | 1817-1905 | 18 |
| 4. Air arabe | Félix Le Couppey | 1811-1887 | 19 |
| 5. Bärentanz | Robert Schumann | 1810-1856 | 20 |
| 6. Prelude | Carl Reinecke | 1824-1910 | 21 |
| 7. Stückchen | Robert Schumann | 1810-1856 | 22 |
| 8. Gavotte | Cornelius Gurlitt | 1820-1901 | 23 |
| 9. Petite pièce | Vincent d'Indy | 1851-1931 | 24 |
| 10. Melodie | Robert Schumann | 1810-1856 | 24 |
| 11. Soldatenmarsch | Robert Schumann | 1810-1856 | 25 |
| 12. Arabesque | Johann Burgmüller | 1806-1874 | 26 |
| 13. Allegro non Troppo | Cornelius Gurlitt | 1820-1901 | 27 |
| 14. Les Pifferari | Charles Gounod | 1818-1893 | 28 |
| 15. Stolzer Reitersmann | Robert Fuchs | 1847-1927 | 30 |
| 16. Étude No. 17 | Félix Le Couppey | 1811-1887 | 31 |
| 17. Étude No. 15 | Félix Le Couppey | 1811-1887 | 32 |
| 18. Andante in F Minor | Bedrich Smetana | 1824-1884 | 34 |
| 19. Through the Desert | Sergei Bortkiewicz | 1877-1952 | 34 |
| 20. Bourrée | Frédéric Chopin | 1810-1849 | 35 |
| 21. Haschemann | Robert Schumann | 1810-1856 | 36 |
| 22. The Doll's Illness | Peter Tchaikovsky | 1840-1893 | 37 |
| 23. Banges Herzelein | Robert Fuchs | 1847-1927 | 38 |
| 24. Op. 27 No. 3 | Robert Volkmann | 1815-1883 | 39 |
| 25. Polka | Mikhail Glinka | 1804-1857 | 40 |
| 26. Allegretto | Nicolai Rimsky-Korsakov | 1844-1908 | 40 |
| 27. The New Doll | Peter Tchaikovsky | 1840-1893 | 42 |
| 28. Invention | Sergey Lyapunov | 1859-1924 | 44 |
| 29. Kuckuck im Versteck | Robert Schumann | 1810-1856 | 45 |
| 30. Op. 27 No. 11 | Robert Volkmann | 1815-1883 | 46 |

## Introduction

The present collections of piano pieces are the result of teaching pupils of all ages and abilities. Whilst anthologies are, inevitably, a personal selection of works, it has been my intention to include repertoire that is both idiomatically written and pianistically useful.

This selection of pieces also contains some deliberate challenges to the piano student. Playing works with three sharps or four flats at Grade 2 level is unusual but not impossible. As such, I have been guided less by the systems created by examination boards and more by my own practical experience as a teacher.

Stylistically, I have attempted to present a broad range of compositional styles of the romantic period and I have searched for original material by some of the 19th century's most influential piano composers. For example, works by Schumann, Chopin, Smetana, Tchaikovsky and Rimsky-Korsakov can be found at Grade 2 level in the hope of introducing piano students to their music as soon as possible.

From a technical point of view, I decided to include music that is so diverse that the student is able to develop a broad range of different technical skills, from finger agility to silent finger changes on a note, from playing chordal textures to linear passage work and part-playing.

The teaching notes included in this book are designed to help the student by offering some ideas on how to practise or on how to approach a particular piece. The commentary cannot, and is not meant to, replace the collaborative spirit that student and teacher share in a lesson.

I hope that some of the repertoire in this anthology can provide students with the intrinsic motivation to practise and thus enable them to enjoy the process of music-making through study and performance.

Nils Franke

## Introduction

Ces recueils de pièces pour piano sont l'aboutissement de mon expérience d'enseignant auprès d'élèves de tous âges aux dons plus ou moins développés. Les anthologies reflètent inévitablement les choix personnels de leur auteur, et j'ai voulu rassembler ici un répertoire présentant à la fois une écriture idiomatique et une utilité d'un point de vue pianistique.

Cette sélection contient intentionnellement quelques défis pour les élèves pianistes. Jouer des œuvres avec trois dièses ou quatre bémols à la clé en premier cycle est inhabituel, mais pas impossible. Sur ce plan, je me suis laissé guider moins par les recommandations des comités de concours que par mon expérience d'enseignant.

Sur le plan stylistique, j'ai tenté de présenter un large éventail de styles issus de la période romantique, et ai orienté mes recherches sur du matériel original provenant des compositeurs les plus marquants du XIXe siècle. Je propose par exemple des œuvres de Schumann, Chopin, Smetana, Tchaïkovski et Rimski-Korsakov dès le premier cycle, dans l'objectif de sensibiliser les élèves à la musique de ces compositeurs le plus tôt possible.

Sur le plan technique, j'ai décidé d'inclure de la musique très variée, afin que les élèves aient la possibilité de développer toutes sortes de facultés techniques — agilité des doigts ou changement de doigts silencieux sur une note, — et d'aborder différents types d'écriture dans des passages harmoniques, linéaires ou polyphoniques.

Les notes pédagogiques jointes à ce recueil sont destinées à aider les élèves en leur proposant des idées sur le travail ou sur l'approche spécifique d'une œuvre donnée. Ce commentaire ne peut ni ne prétend remplacer l'esprit de collaboration que partagent le professeur et l'élève au cours d'une leçon.

J'espère que certaines œuvres de cette anthologie pourront procurer aux élèves la motivation intérieure nécessaire à leur travail et leur permettra de prendre plaisir au processus musical par l'étude et l'interprétation.

Nils Franke
(Traduction : Agnès Ausseur)

## Einleitung

Die vorliegende Sammlung von Klavierstücken ist das Ergebnis meiner Lehrtätigkeit mit Schülern jeglichen Alters und Könnens. Obwohl es unvermeidlich ist, dass Sammelbände eine persönliche Auswahl von Stücken sind, war es meine Absicht, idiomatisch geschriebene Repertoirestücke mit pianistisch nützlichen zu verbinden.

Die Stückauswahl beinhaltet außerdem einige bewusste Herausforderungen für den Klavierschüler. Auf Anfängerniveau Stücke mit drei Kreuzen oder vier Bs zu spielen ist ungewöhnlich, aber nicht unmöglich. Daher habe ich mich weniger den Vorgaben von Prüfungskommissionen leiten lassen, als vielmehr von meiner eigenen, praktischen Erfahrung als Lehrer.

Stilistisch habe ich versucht, eine weite Bandbreite an Kompositionsstilen der romantischen Periode vorzustellen. Außerdem habe ich nach Originalmaterial von einigen der einflussreichsten Komponisten für Klavier aus dem 19. Jahrhundert gesucht. So können zum Beispiel Werke von Schumann, Chopin, Smetana, Tschaikowsky und Rimsky-Korsakov auf Anfängerebene gefunden werden, mit dem Ziel, Klavierschüler so früh wie möglich mit ihrer Musik vertraut zu machen.

Unter technischen Gesichtspunkten habe ich mich dafür entschieden, Musik mit einzubeziehen, die so unterschiedlich ist, dass der Schüler ein breites Spektrum an technischen Fähigkeiten entwickeln kann, von Geläufigkeit bis zum stummen Fingerwechsel auf einer Note, vom Spiel akkordischer Strukturen bis zu linearer Passagenarbeit und dem Spielen von zweistimmigen Werken.

Die Anmerkungen zur Erarbeitung in diesem Heft sind darauf ausgelegt, dem Schüler zu helfen, indem er einige Anregungen bekommt, wie er üben oder wie er an ein bestimmtes Stück herangehen kann. Diese Kommentare können nicht und sollen auch nicht den gemeinsamen Arbeitsgeist ersetzen, den Schüler und Lehrer in einer Unterrichtsstunde miteinander teilen.

Ich hoffe, dass ein Teil des Repertoires in dieser Anthologie den Schülern die intrinsische Motivation zum Üben vermittelt und sie dadurch befähigt, den Prozess des Musikmachens durch Studium und Darbietung zu genießen.

Nils Franke
(Übersetzung: Ute Corleis)

# Teaching notes

## Cornelius Gurlitt

*Allegretto Grazioso.* [♩ = 72–76] There are two challenges in this short but effective piece. Musically, lift the dynamic level of bars 9 to 16 above the *p* register of the first and last line. The crescendo in bars 13 to 15 is important, as it reaches its climax on the first beat of bar 16. Even quavers are needed throughout the piece, whichever dynamic you are playing at.                P. 17

*Gavotte.* [♩ = 80–86] This dance is an effective piece for performance. Listen out for the co-ordination between your hands in bars 3, 7, 16 and 23. Quavers and crotchets have to be co-ordinated precisely in these sections.                P. 23

*Allegro non Troppo.* [♩ = 118–124] The key to learning this piece is to reverse the usual right-hand/left-hand balance in favour of the left hand (which has the melody in this study). You can achieve this by first of all replacing a difference in dynamics with a difference in touch. Play the right hand with a light staccato touch and the left hand with a firmer legato sound. Once you have got used to this, aim to hold the right-hand notes for longer whilst still listening to the left-hand line. Eventually the right hand will play legato notes, as will the left hand, but will be on a softer dynamic level than the left.                P. 27

## Félix Le Couppey

*Melody.* [♩. = 72–76] The 6/8 rhythm of this piece demands an even but relaxed left hand with a flexible wrist. Practise the left hand in bars 1 to 8 as chord progressions, similar to bar 9 ff. This will help you find the notes more quickly once you play them as notated. Bars 9 to 16 are the middle section of this piece. They need to be played with a good forte sound without the right hand being overpowered by the left.                P. 17

*Arabian Air.* [♩ = 92–98] This is an excellent piece for promoting independence of hands, as the musical texture of both hands changes quite frequently. To achieve fluency in bars 15 and 23, think about the change of chord in the left hand whilst you play the right-hand semiquavers. That way the left hand is on time when you reach the beginning of the next bar.                P. 19

*Étude No. 17.* [♩. = 80–88] This étude, taken from the composer's *24 Études primaires pour piano pour les petites mains*, further develops skills first learnt in Burgmüller's *Arabesque* (see page 26). In the original edition, first published by Schott, the composer offers a five-bar finger exercise. The study of this supporting exercise is meant to help the student develop the relevant technical skills for learning the piece itself. As in the case of Burgmüller's *Arabesque*, Le Couppey also provides opportunities for the left hand to develop the same skills as the right hand.                P. 31

*Étude No. 15* [♩. = 128–136] further develops skills first encountered in Gounod's *Les Pifferari*. As such it may be a suitable alternative for number 14 of this anthology.                P. 32

## Fritz Spindler

*Song without Words.* [♩. = 84–88] Throughout the piece, keep the left hand softer than the right in order for the melody to shine. This piece can work well at different tempi, depending on whether you hear this as being three notes per bar or as one note per bar.                P. 18

## Robert Schumann

*Bear Dance.* [♩ = 96–104] Getting used to playing with hands so far apart from each other is the first step when practising hands together. Please note that Schumann did not provide any dynamic markings for the beginning of this piece. This is an excellent opportunity for experimenting with dynamics before deciding which way to play this. *Bear Dance, Haschemann* and *Cuckoo in Hiding* (see below) are pieces originally intended for the *Album for the Young*, op. 68. However, Schumann withdrew all three pieces before publication!                P. 20

*Little Piece.* [♩ = 116–128] There are two melody lines to look out for in this piece. The right hand which has the main melody is supported by the first and third quaver of every group of quavers in the left hand. This means that you can practise the left hand in two different ways: firstly, as a group of even quavers and secondly with more emphasis on the first and third quaver, whilst keeping the second and fourth quavers soft.                P. 22

*Melody.* [♩ = 118–126] Treat the left hand similarly to that of *Little Piece*. However, as a piece, *Melody* is a little bit more difficult than *Little Piece* because the melodic lines are less obvious. Also, in bar 8 connect the F on the 3rd beat of the bar to the D, the last quaver in the bar. This means that the other quavers on beats 3 and 4 have to be played rather softly, so that the melody line can come through.                P. 24

*Soldiers' March* [♩ = 70–76] is great fun to practise! Make the semiquaver as late and as short as you can, so that the rhythm is sharp and precise. In bar 9, the composer changes from quavers to crotchets, and then back to quavers in bar 11. Aim to make those different sounds (and the frequent changes that follow) very clear.                P. 25

*Haschemann* [♩ = 126–132] certainly requires even finger work and the ability to play lightly and quickly. Given the repetitive patterns, this piece could be used for memory work which will certainly help a potential performance situation.                P. 36

*Cuckoo in Hiding.* [♩ = 96–108] The main challenges of this piece are the sustaining of direction at such a quiet dynamic with so many rests and the frequency of hand-position changes. In bars 9 to 12 the lower line of the left hand plays a counter-melody to the right hand.                P. 45

## Carl Reinecke

*Prelude.* [♩ = 92–98] To learn the changing positions of the right hand, you might find it useful to practise each group of right hand quavers in bars 1 to 7 as chords. Doing so will greatly enhance the fluency of your performance. Look out for the crescendo and decrescendo marks which need to be carefully controlled from the left hand.                P. 21

## Vincent d'Indy

*Little Piece.* [♩ = 92–96] This is an interesting piece harmonically. Both hands play seemingly independent melodic lines, yet when you put hands together, the harmonies make perfect sense. Follow the composer's phrase marks when you practise this. This gives you smaller, self-contained sections to work on.                P. 24

## Johann Burgmüller

*Arabesque.* [♩ = 128–136] An excellent piece for performance,

*Arabesque* trains both your right and left hand to equal degree. Just look at the semiquaver runs in the right hand in bars 3 to 6, and the semiquaver patterns in the left hand in bars 11 to 15. When choosing a tempo for the opening, play through bar 3. Here you can establish the basic crotchet speed which you can then apply to the beginning. If you haven't already done so, use the right pedal in the last bar of this piece. The fermata gives you time to press down the right pedal after the chord has been played. The sound you get from the piano at that point should be much fuller than if you didn't use the pedal. When you want to release the pedal, let fingers and foot go at the same time. P. 26

### Charles Gounod

*The Bagpipers.* [♩ = 126–136] This is another excellent piece for performance. To achieve the best possible co-ordination between both hands, you might want to practise this in two different ways. At first, listen to the right hand and fit the left hand to the melody line of the right. The second stage is to reverse the process. This may make the piece sound differently, both in terms of balance and fluency. The benefit of practising like this is that a) you get to know the melodic lines of both hands and b) hand co-ordination should be quite accurate. P. 28

### Robert Fuchs

*Proud Horseman.* [♩ = 98–104] Placing the chords of the left hand between the notes of the right hand can, at first, be a challenge. Keep the chords light in touch when you start to practise hands together, so that they don't interfere with either pulse or balance. The change in texture in the left hand of bar 18 does take some getting used to. When practising, play the first and fourth quaver of the bar a bit firmer to help with finger co-ordination and musical flow. P. 30

*Sad at Heart.* [♩ = 112–118] Once you have learnt the notes, do experiment with the overall tempo. 'Etwas bewegt' quite literally means 'with a little bit of movement'. In bar 15, position the right hand thumb near the D before you play the preceding G sharp. P. 38

### Bedrich Smetana

*Andante in F Minor.* [♩ = 50–56] This short album leaf dates from 1880. The left hand of this work needs careful attention, so that the melodic lines can be heard clearly. Smetana's piano music includes many individual and short character pieces, of which this probably the shortest. The pedal marks are the composer's own. P. 34

### Sergei Bortkiewicz

*Through the Desert.* [♩ = 102–108] Bortkiewicz's 'The Little Wanderer', from which this piece was taken, was first published in 1923 and is undoubtedly the result of his work as a piano teacher. In this set, Bortkiewicz portrays various aspects of travel as well as the countries that the little wanderer visits. The piece is a beautifully written two-part work which helps develop this aspect of part playing. P. 34

### Frédéric Chopin

*Bourrée.* [♩ = 120–128] This piece, first published by Schott in 1968 and edited by Ates Orga, is the composer's harmonization of a folk melody. Chopin did not intend for this to be published, as the absence of articulation and dynamics seems to suggest. It is this very fact that makes this such an interesting

piece for teaching purposes, as there is room for experimentation and decision-making which will involve both student and teacher. Smaller hands may need to re-arrange the chords in the left hand in bars 11 and 15. Octaves can be broken, but the last chord in bar 15 may need to be played without D, whilst the C sharp is moved down one octave. P. 35

### Peter Tchaikovsky

Both pieces by Tchaikovsky are taken from a collection of 24 pieces entitled *Children's Album*, op. 39. Tchaikovsky's subtitle, *Collection of easy pieces for children à la Schumann*, clearly indicates that Schumann's *Album for the Young* op. 68 was the inspiration for his own work.

*The Doll's Illness.* [♩ = 50–54] Separate hand practice might be useful in the early stages, but you will only get an accurate impression of this piece when you start to practise with both hands. Depending on the overall sound you want to create, the melody line can either dominate over the other parts or it could be part of the overall texture. The use of the right pedal is not notated but almost certainly an important part of this piece. P.37

*The New Doll.* [♩ = 96–104] This piece is clearly right-hand-led. Fit the left-hand accompaniment to support the melodic line in the right. P. 42

### Robert Volkmann

Both pieces by Volkmann are part of a collection of 13 pieces called 'Grandmother's Songs' op. 27, first published by Schott. *Op. 27 no. 3* [♩ = 84–88] is an expressive miniature that gives you the opportunity to practise slow legato playing. P. 39

*Op. 27 no. 11* [♩ = 76–80] is a show piece that requires good left hand dexterity and clear co-ordination skills between the hands, particularly in bars 20 to 33. P. 46

### Mikhail Glinka

*Polka.* [♩ = 100–104] A moderately lively piece, there are several aspects to listen out for. Firstly, do make a difference between the legato and staccato articulation in bar 3 and the legato markings in bar 7. Secondly, keep the left hand detached throughout. It makes a good contrast to the right hand which is predominantly legato. And thirdly, in bar 3 you can use the thumb of your left hand for G and A by slightly moving it sideways. P. 40

### Nicolai Rimsky-Korsakov

*Allegretto.* [♩ = 92–98] The outer parts of this piece further develop the two-part playing skills first encountered in Bortkiewicz's *Through the Desert* (page 34). The middle section in bars 33 to 48 contains two octaves which can be played with both hands, subject to maintaining the overall tempo. P. 40

### Sergey Lyapunov

*Invention.* [♩ = 84–92] Following on from Bortkiewicz's and Rimsky-Korsakov's pieces (pp. 34 and 40) here is another chance to develop part playing, but this time in a more demanding key. In bars 9 to 14 follow the phrase marks of each line to learn this sequence in smaller, one to one-and-a-half bar units. Dynamically, the music only moves between *mf* and *p*. P. 44

Nils Franke

# Notes pédagogiques

### Cornelius Gurlitt

*Allegretto Grazioso.* [♩ = 72–76] Cette pièce courte, mais efficace présente deux défis. Musicalement, il s'agit d'élever la dynamique des mesures 9 à 16 au dessus du registre piano des première et dernière lignes. Le *crescendo* des mesures 13 à 15 est important et atteint son apogée sur le premier temps de la mesure 16. Les croches seront régulières tout au long de la pièce, quelle que soit la dynamique requise.                                    P. 17

*Gavotte.* [♩ = 80–86] Cette danse fait son petit effet lorsqu'elle est jouée en public. Soyez attentif à la coordination entre vos deux mains aux mesures 3, 7, 16 et 23. Les croches et noires doivent être parfaitement synchrones dans ces passages.          P. 23

*Allegro non Troppo.* [♩ = 118–124] La clé pour l'interprétation de cette pièce réside dans l'inversion de l'équilibre habituel main droite – main gauche en faveur de cette dernière (qui a la mélodie dans cette étude). Vous y parviendrez tout d'abord en remplaçant la différence de dynamique par une différence de toucher. Appliquez un léger *staccato* à la main droite et un *legato* bien affirmé à la main gauche. Lorsque vous vous serez habitué à cette manière de jouer, efforcez-vous de tenir un peu plus longtemps les notes de la main droite tout en écoutant la ligne de la main gauche. Pour finir, la main droite jouera également *legato*, mais dans une dynamique plus douce que la main gauche.          P. 27

### Félix Le Couppey

*Mélodie.* [♩. = 72–76] Le rythme en 6/8 de cette pièce demande une main gauche régulière, bien que détendue, ainsi qu'un poignet souple. Travaillez la main gauche des mesures 1 à 8 sous la forme d'une succession d'accords similaire à celle des mesures 9 et suivantes. Cela vous aidera à trouver les notes plus rapidement lorsque vous les jouerez comme elles sont écrites. Les mesures 9 à 16 représentent la partie centrale de cette pièce. Elles demandent à être jouées *forte* sans toutefois que la main droite soit submergée par la gauche.          P. 17

*Air arabe.* [♩ = 92–98] Du fait du changement fréquent de matériau musical aux deux mains, cette pièce est parfaite pour améliorer l'indépendance des mains. Afin d'obtenir un jeu fluide aux mesures 15 et 23, pensez au changement d'accord de la main gauche pendant que vous jouez les doubles-croches de la main droite. De cette façon, la main gauche sera au rendez-vous lorsque vous atteindrez le début de la mesure suivante.          P. 19

*Étude n° 17.* [♩ = 80–88] Cette étude, tirée des *24 Études primaires de piano pour les petites mains* du compositeur, développe plus avant les savoir-faire abordés dans l'*Arabesque* de Burgmüller (voir page 26). Dans l'édition originale publiée initialement par Schott, le compositeur propose un exercice de 5 mesures pour les doigts. Ce travail préparatoire est destiné à aider l'élève à développer les qualités techniques nécessaires à l'exécution de la pièce proprement dite. Tout comme pour Burgmüller dans son *Arabesque*, Le Couppey permet ici à la main gauche de développer les mêmes qualités que la main droite.          P. 31

*Étude n° 15.* [♩ = 128–136] Développe plus avant les compétences rencontrées pour la première fois dans *Les Pifferari* de Gounod. Elle peut ainsi constituer une alternative tout à fait adaptée au numéro 14 de la présente anthologie.          P. 32

### Fritz Spindler

*Chanson sans paroles.* [♩ = 84–88] Tout au long de la pièce, pensez à garder la main gauche moins forte que la main droite afin de mettre la mélodie en valeur. Cette pièce fonctionne très bien à différents tempi selon que vous entendez trois pulsations par mesure ou une seule.          P. 18

### Robert Schumann

*La danse de l'ours.* [♩ = 96–104] S'habituer à jouer les mains très éloignées l'une de l'autre est la première étape du jeu mains ensemble. Il est à noter que Schumann n'a donné aucune indication de dynamique pour le début de cette pièce. C'est une excellente occasion de tester différentes nuances avant de décider de quelle manière vous allez la jouer. *La danse de l'ours*, *Haschemann* et le *Coucou dans sa cachette* (voir ci dessous) sont des pièces destinées à l'origine à son *Album pour la jeunesse* op. 68. Cependant, Schumann les a supprimées juste avant la publication de l'album.          P. 20

*Petite pièce.* [♩ = 116–128] Dans ce morceau, votre attention devra se concentrer principalement sur deux lignes mélodiques. La main droite joue la mélodie principale, elle-même soutenue par la première et la troisième croche de chaque groupe de croches de la main gauche. Par conséquent, vous avez la possibilité de travailler la main gauche de deux manières différentes : soit en jouant les groupes de croches de manière régulière, ou alors en accentuant la première et la troisième croche plus que la seconde et la quatrième.          P. 22

*Mélodie.* [♩ = 118–126] Le traitement de la main gauche est similaire à celui de la *Petite pièce* qui précède. Cependant, la *Mélodie* est globalement plus difficile, car les lignes mélodiques sont moins évidentes à suivre. À la mesure 8, il faudra également bien lier le *fa* du troisième temps au *ré*, dernière croche de la mesure. Cela signifie que les autres croches du troisième et quatrième temps seront jouées plus doucement afin de permettre à la ligne mélodique de s'affirmer.          P. 24

*La marche du soldat* [♩ = 70–76] est très amusante à jouer. La double-croche doit être jouée le plus tard et le plus brièvement possible afin que le rythme soit bien précis et marqué. À la mesure 9, le compositeur passe des croches aux noires pour revenir aux croches à la mesure 11. Veillez à bien différencier les sonorités (ainsi que les changements fréquents qui suivent).          P. 25

*Haschemann* [♩ = 126–132] nécessite un travail des doigts très régulier et la capacité de jouer avec légèreté et rapidité. Compte tenu de la répétitivité des motifs, ce morceau pourra être utilisé pour travailler la mémoire en prévision d'une situation de concert potentielle.          P. 36

*Le coucou dans sa cachette.* [♩ = 96–108] La dynamique très douce et la présence de nombreux silences rendent peu aisé le maintien d'une intention musicale constante. De fréquents changements de position des mains constituent une difficulté supplémentaire de ce morceau. Dans les mesures 9 à 12, la ligne la plus grave de la main gauche joue un contre-chant par rapport à la main droite.          P. 45

### Carl Reinecke

*Prélude.* [♩ = 92–98] Afin de maîtriser les changements de position à la main droite, vous trouverez peut-être utile de vous entraîner à jouer chaque groupe de croches de la main droite des mesures 1 à 7 sous forme d'accords. De cette manière, vous améliorerez sensiblement la fluidité de votre jeu. Soyez attentif aux *crescendo* et *decrescendo* qui doivent être soigneusement contrôlés à la main gauche. P. 21

### Vincent d'Indy

*Petite pièce*. [♩ = 92–96] Ce morceau présente un intérêt particulier du point de vue harmonique. Les deux mains semblent jouer des lignes mélodiques indépendantes, mais les harmonies prendront tout leur sens lorsque vous les mettrez ensemble. Suivez les indications de phrasé données par le compositeur en travaillant cette pièce. Cela vous permettra de travailler des fragments plus courts et autonomes. P. 24

### Johann Burgmüller

*Arabesque*. [♩ = 128–136] Très appréciée en audition, cette *Arabesque* permet de faire travailler autant la main gauche que la main droite. Prenez soin cependant d'être attentif aux doubles-croches de la main droite aux mesures 3 à 6, et à celles de la main gauche aux mesures 11 à 15. Lorsque vous choisirez un tempo pour le démarrage, commencez par jouer la mesure 3. Cela vous permettra d'établir la vitesse de base à laquelle vous réaliserez les croches. Si vous ne l'avez pas encore fait, utilisez la pédale de droite du piano dans la dernière mesure de ce morceau. Le point d'orgue vous donnera le temps d'appuyer sur la pédale après avoir joué l'accord. Le son que vous obtiendrez ainsi devrait être plus plein que si vous n'aviez pas utilisé la pédale. Lorsque vous voulez la lâcher, levez simultanément les doigts et le pied. P. 26

### Charles Gounod

*Les Pifferari*. [♩. = 126–136] Encore une pièce tout à fait adaptée à une prestation publique. Deux axes de travail vous permettront d'obtenir la meilleure coordination possible des deux mains. Écoutez d'abord la main droite et calez la main gauche sur la ligne mélodique de la main droite. La seconde étape consiste à inverser le processus. Cela fera peut-être sonner la pièce différemment, à la fois en termes de fluidité et d'équilibre des voix. Travailler de cette manière présente deux avantages. D'une part, vous vous familiariserez avec les lignes mélodiques des deux mains et d'autre part, la coordination des mains sera plus précise. P. 28

### Robert Fuchs

*Fier cavalier*. [♩. = 98–104] Au début, vous trouverez peut-être difficile de placer les accords de la main gauche entre les notes de la main droite. Lorsque vous commencerez à travailler mains ensemble, pensez à gardez la main légère sur les accords afin qu'ils n'interfèrent ni sur la pulsation ni sur l'équilibre sonore. Le changement de texture à la main gauche de la mesure 18 nécessite une certaine habitude. Lorsque vous travaillez, accentuez légèrement la première et la quatrième croche des mesures afin de faciliter la coordination et le flux musical. P. 30

*Un cœur triste*. [♩ = 112–118] Lorsque vous aurez appris les notes, faites quelques essais sur le tempo général. 'Etwas bewegt' signifie littéralement 'un peu animé'. À la mesure 15, positionnez le pouce près du *ré* avant de jouer le *sol* dièse qui précède. P. 38

### Bedrich Smetana

*Andante en fa mineur*. [♩ = 50–56] Cette courte page est extraite d'un album daté de 1880. La main gauche de ce morceau requerra une grande attention afin de laisser entendre la ligne mélodique avec clarté. La musique pour piano de Smetana comprend de nombreuses pièces de caractère assez brèves, mais celle-ci est sans doute la plus courte dans son genre. Les indications de pédale sont celles du compositeur. P. 34

### Sergei Bortkiewicz

*À travers les steppes*. [♩ = 102–108] *Le petit voyageur* de Bortkiewicz, dont cette page est extraite, a été publié pour la première fois en 1923 et représente sans nul doute l'aboutissement de son activité de professeur de piano. Bortkiewicz y décrit le voyage sous différents aspects ainsi que les pays visités par le petit voyageur. Il s'agit ici d'une pièce à deux voix merveilleusement écrite qui permet de développer cet aspect du jeu polyphonique. P. 34

### Frédéric Chopin

*Bourrée*. [♩ = 120–128] Ce morceau, publié par Schott pour la première fois en 1968 et édité par Ates Orga, est l'harmonisation par le compositeur d'une mélodie folklorique. Chopin n'avait pas l'intention de la publier, comme semble le suggérer l'absence d'indications d'articulation et de dynamique. C'est justement ce qui la rend si intéressante dans la perspective de l'enseignement, car cela laisse la place à des expériences et des prises de décision qui impliquent à la fois l'élève et le professeur. Les petites mains nécessiteront peut-être de réaménager les accords de la main gauche aux mesures 11 et 15. Les octaves peuvent être arpégées, mais le dernier accord de la mesure 15 devra peut-être être joué sans le *ré* tandis que le *do* dièse sera joué une octave plus bas. P. 35

### Piotr Tchaïkovski

Les deux pièces de Tchaïkovski sont tirées d'un recueil intitulé *Album pour les enfants* op. 39. Le sous-titre donné par Tchaïkovski, *Recueil de pièces faciles à la Schumann*, indique clairement que l'*Album pour la jeunesse* op. 68 de Schumann a inspiré son travail.

*La maladie de la poupée*. [♩ = 50–54] Il sera utile de commencer par un travail mains séparées, mais vous n'aurez une vision précise de cette pièce que lorsque vous commencerez à travailler mains ensemble. En fonction de la sonorité que vous souhaiterez créer, la ligne mélodique pourra dominer les autres parties ou alors s'intégrer dans le matériau général. L'utilisation de la pédale de droite n'est pas notée, mais jouera certainement un rôle important dans l'interprétation de cette pièce. P. 37

*La nouvelle poupée*. [♩ = 96–104] Cette pièce est clairement conduite par la main droite. Adaptez l'accompagnement de la main gauche afin de soutenir la ligne mélodique de la main droite. P. 42

### Robert Volkmann

Ces deux pièces de Volkmann font partie d'un recueil de treize pièces intitulé *Les chansons de grand-mère* op. 27, publié initialement chez Schott.

L'opus 27 n° 3 [♩ = 84–88] est une miniature expressive qui vous donne l'occasion d'exercer un jeu lent et *legato*. P. 39

L'opus 27 n° 11 [♩. = 76–80] est une pièce brillante qui requiert une bonne dextérité de la main gauche et une coordination claire entre les deux mains, notamment entre les mesures 20 à 33. P. 46

**Mikhail Glinka**

*Polka.* [♩ = 100–104] Pièce modérément animée dont plusieurs aspects doivent retenir votre attention. Tout d'abord, il faudra faire la différence entre les *legato* et *staccato* de la mesure 3 et le *legato* de la mesure 7. Ensuite, la main gauche doit rester détachée tout au long de la pièce. Elle constitue un bon contraste par rapport à la main droite qui est principalement *legato*. Enfin, à la mesure 3, vous pouvez utiliser le pouce de la main gauche pour jouer le *sol* et le *la* en effectuant un léger mouvement latéral.                     P. 40

**Nicolaï Rimski-Korsakov**

*Allegretto.* [♩ = 92–98] Les parties extrêmes de cette pièce continuent à développer le jeu à deux voix rencontré pour la première fois dans *À travers les steppes* de Bortkiewicz (page 34). La section centrale des mesures 33 à 48 comprend deux séries d'octaves. Celles-ci peuvent être jouées avec les deux mains, à condition de maintenir le tempo général.                     P. 40

**Sergey Lyapunov**

*Invention.* [♩ = 84–92] Dans la continuité des pièces de Bortkiewicz et Rimski-Korsakov (pp. 34 et 40), voici une nouvelle possibilité de développer le jeu polyphonique, mais cette fois dans une tonalité un peu plus difficile. De la mesure 9 à la mesure 14, suivez les indications de phrasé de chaque partie afin d'apprendre cette séquence par unités plus petites d'une mesure à une mesure et demie. D'un point de vue dynamique, la musique reste cantonnée entre le *mf* et le *p*.                     P. 44

Nils Franke

# Anmerkungen zur Erarbeitung

**Cornelius Gurlitt**

*Allegretto Grazioso.* [♩ = 72–76] In diesem kurzen, aber wirkungsvollen Stück gibt es zwei Herausforderungen. Hebe die Dynamik der Takte 9 bis 16 musikalisch über das *p* der ersten und letzten Zeile. Das Crescendo in den Takten 13 bis 15 ist wichtig, da es seinen Höhepunkt auf dem ersten Schlag von Takt 16 erreicht. Außerdem braucht man im ganzen Stück gleichmäßige Achtelnoten, ganz egal, mit welcher Dynamik man spielt.     S. 17

*Gavotte.* [♩ = 80–86] Dieser Tanz ist ein sehr wirkungsvolles Aufführungsstück. Achte besonders auf die Koordination beider Hände in den Takten 3, 7, 16 und 23. Die Achtel- und die Viertelnoten müssen in diesen Teilen genau aufeinander abgestimmt werden.                     S. 23

*Allegro non Troppo.* [♩ = 118–124] Der Schlüssel zum Erlernen dieses Stückes liegt darin, die übliche Balance der rechten und linken Hand zu Gunsten der linken Hand umzukehren (die in diesem Stück die Melodie spielt). Das kann man erreichen, indem man als erstes eine dynamische Differenzierung durch eine Differenzierung im Anschlag ersetzt. Spiele die rechte Hand mit einem leichten Staccato-Anschlag und die linke Hand mit einem festeren Legato-Ton. Sobald du dich daran gewöhnt hast, ist dein nächstes Ziel die Noten der rechten Hand zu verlängern, während man gleichzeitig immer noch der Linie der linken Hand zuhört. Schließlich spielt die rechte Hand, genauso wie die linke, Legato-Noten, aber auf einer weicheren, dynamischen Ebene als die linke.                     S. 27

**Félix Le Couppey**

*Melodie.* [♩ = 72–76] Der 6/8-Rhythmus dieses Stückes erfordert eine gleichmäßige, aber entspannte linke Hand mit einem beweglichen Handgelenk. Übe die linke Hand in den Takten 1 bis 8 als Abfolge von Akkorden, ähnlich wie im Takt 9 ff. Das wird dir dabei helfen, die Noten schneller zu finden, wenn du sie wie notiert spielst. Die Takte 9 bis 16 sind der Mittelteil dieses Musikstückes. Sie müssen in einem guten forte gespielt werden, aber ohne dass die rechte Hand von der linken übertönt wird.     S. 17

*Arabische Weise.* [♩ = 92–98] Das ist ein ausgezeichnetes Stück, um die Unabhängigkeit der Hände zu üben, da die musikalische Struktur beider Hände recht häufig wechselt. Denke an den Akkordwechsel in der linken Hand, während du die Sechzehntel in der rechten Hand spielst, um in den Takten 15 und 23 Geläufigkeit zu erlangen. Auf diese Weise ist die linke Hand pünktlich, wenn du den Anfang des nächsten Taktes erreichst.     S. 19

*Étude No. 17.* [♩ = 80–88] Diese Etüde, den *24 Études primaires pour piano pour les petites mains* des Komponisten entnommen, entwickelt die Fähigkeiten weiter, die man erstmals in Burgmüllers *Arabesque* (s. S. 12) gelernt hat. In der Erstausgabe, die zuerst von Schott veröffentlicht wurde, bietet der Komponist eine fünftaktige Fingerübung an. Die Beschäftigung mit dieser unterstützenden Übung soll dem Schüler helfen, die erforderlichen technischen Fähigkeiten für das Erlernen des Stückes zu trainieren. Genau wie im Falle von Burgmüllers *Arabesque* bietet Le Couppey Möglichkeiten für die linke Hand an, die gleichen Fähigkeiten wie die rechte Hand zu entwickeln.     S. 31

Die *Étude No. 15* [♩ = 128–136] bildet Fähigkeiten weiter aus, denen man zum ersten Mal in Gounods *Les Pifferari* begegnete. So gesehen kann sie eine passende Alternative zur Nummer 14 dieser Anthologie darstellen.     S. 32

**Fritz Spindler**

*Song without Words* (Lied ohne Worte). [♩ = 84–88] Spiele die linke Hand im ganzen Stück weicher als die rechte, damit die Melodie glänzen kann. Dieses Musikstück klingt in verschiedenen Tempi gut. Es kommt nur darauf an, wie man sie hört – als drei Noten pro Takt oder nur als eine Note pro Takt.     S. 18

**Robert Schumann**

*Bärentanz.* [♩ = 96–104] Sich daran zu gewöhnen, dass die Hände so weit auseinander liegen ist der erste Schritt, wenn man beide Hände zusammen übt. Beachte bitte, dass Schumann keine Dynamik für den Anfang des Stückes vorgibt. Das ist eine ausgezeichnete Gelegenheit, mit unterschiedlicher Dynamik herumzuexperimentieren, bevor man entscheidet, auf welche Weise man ihn spielen will. Der *Bärentanz*, *Haschemann* und der *Kuckuck im Versteck* (siehe unten) waren ursprünglich für das *Album für die Jugend, op. 68* vorgesehen. Vor der Veröffentlichung zog Schumann allerdings alle drei Stücke wieder zurück!     S. 20

*Stückchen.* [♩ = 116–128] In diesem Stück gibt es zwei Melodielinien, auf die man achten sollte. Die rechte Hand, die die Hauptmelodie spielt, wird in der linken Hand von der ersten und dritten Achtelnote jeder Achtelnotengruppe unterstützt. Das bedeutet, dass man die linke Hand auf zwei unterschiedliche Arten üben kann: einmal als eine Gruppe gleichmäßiger Achtel und zum anderen mit einer stärkeren Betonung auf der ersten und dritten Achtel, wobei man die zweite und vierte Achtel leise spielt. S. 22

*Melodie.* [♩ = 118–126] Behandle die linke Hand ähnlich wie im *Stückchen*. Als Ganzes gesehen ist die *Melodie* allerdings ein bisschen schwieriger als das *Stückchen*, weil die melodischen Linien weniger offensichtlich sind. Binde in Takt 8 das F auf dem dritten Schlag an das D, das letzte Achtel des Taktes. Das bedeutet, dass die anderen Achtel der Schläge 3 und 4 ziemlich leise gespielt werden müssen, damit die Melodielinie durchklingt. S. 24

Es macht viel Spaß, den *Soldatenmarsch* [♩ = 70–76] zu üben! Spiele die Sechzehntel so spät und so kurz wie möglich, so dass der Rhythmus kurz und präzise ist. In Takt 9 wechselt der Komponist von Achtel- zu Viertelnoten und wieder zurück in Takt 11. Nimm dir vor, diese unterschiedlichen Klänge (und die häufigen Wechsel, die folgen) sehr deutlich zu machen. S. 25

Der *Haschemann* [♩ = 126–132] erfordert auf jeden Fall eine sehr gleichmäßige Fingerarbeit und die Fähigkeit, leicht und schnell zu spielen. Aufgrund der sich wiederholenden Strukturen könnte man dieses Musikstück als Gedächtnistraining verwenden, was einer möglichen Aufführungssituation bestimmt helfen würde. S. 36

*Kuckuck im Versteck.* [♩ = 96–108] Die wichtigste Herausforderung dieses Stückes ist es, bei solch einer ruhigen Dynamik die Zielrichtung aufrecht zu erhalten, mit so vielen Pausen und Handpositionswechseln. In den Takten 9 bis 12 spielt die linke Hand eine Gegenmelodie zur rechten Hand. S. 45

### Carl Reinecke
*Präludium.* [♩ = 92–98] Um die Lagewechsel der rechten Hand zu erlernen, könnte es sinnvoll sein, jede Achtelgruppe der Takte 1 bis 7 in der rechten Hand als Akkord zu üben. Auf diese Weise wird der Fluss der Darbietung stark verbessert werden. Beachte die Crescendo- und Decrescendo-Anweisungen, die von der linken Hand sorgfältig kontrolliert werden müssen. S. 21

### Vincent d'Indy
*Petite pièce* (Kleines Stück). [♩ = 92–96] Dies ist harmonisch gesehen ein interessantes Stück. Beide Hände spielen anscheinend voneinander unabhängige melodische Linien, wenn man jedoch die Hände zusammenlegt, ergeben sich sinnvolle Harmonien. Halte dich beim Üben an die Artikulationsbögen des Komponisten. Dadurch erhältst du kleinere, in sich abgeschlossene Teile, an denen du arbeiten kannst. S. 24

### Johann Burgmüller
*Arabesque.* [♩ = 128–136] Für Aufführungen hervorragend geeignet, übt die *Arabesque* sowohl die rechte als auch die linke Hand zu gleichen Teilen. Schaue dir nur die Sechzehntelläufe der rechten Hand in den Takten 3 bis 6 und die Sechzehntelmuster in der linken Hand der Takte 11 bis 15 an. Spiele Takt 3 durch, wenn du ein Tempo für die Eröffnung wählst. Mit Takt 3 kannst du das Grundtempo der Viertel festlegen, um es dann auf den Anfang zu übertragen. Benutze im letzten Takt des Stückes das rechte Pedal, falls du es nicht schon tust. Die Fermate gibt dir die Zeit, das rechte Pedal zu treten, nachdem der Akkord angeschlagen wurde. Der Klang, den du an dieser Stelle vom Klavier erhältst, sollte deutlich voller sein als ohne Pedal. Hebe Finger und Fuß gleichzeitig an, wenn du vom Pedal heruntergehen willst. S. 26

### Charles Gounod
*Les Pifferari* (Die Dudelsackspieler). [♩. = 126–136] Ein weiteres ausgezeichnetes Aufführungsstück. Um die bestmögliche Koordination zwischen beiden Händen zu erhalten, sollte man dieses Stück auf zwei unterschiedliche Arten üben. Lausche zunächst der rechten Hand und passe die linke Hand der Melodielinie an. Im zweiten Schritt wird der Prozess umgedreht. Auf diese Weise sollte das Stück sowohl in Bezug auf die Balance als auch den Fluss ganz anders klingen. Der Vorteil dieser Art zu üben ist, dass man a) die melodischen Linien beider Hände kennen lernt und b) die Handkoordination ziemlich genau sein sollte. S. 28

### Robert Fuchs
*Stolzer Reitersmann.* [♩. = 98–104] Die Akkorde der linken Hand zwischen die Noten der rechten zu platzieren, kann anfänglich eine Herausforderung darstellen. Wenn du beginnst, beide Hände zusammen zu üben, belasse die Akkorde leicht im Anschlag, um weder den Grundschlag noch die Balance zu stören. An die veränderte Struktur der linken Hand ab Takt 18 muss man sich erst gewöhnen. Spiele die erste und vierte Achtelnote eines Taktes beim Üben etwas lauter, um die Koordinierung der Finger und den musikalischen Fluss zu unterstützen. S. 30

*Banges Herzelein.* [♩ = 112–118] Experimentiere mit dem Gesamttempo, nachdem du die Noten gelernt hast. Bringe den Daumen der rechten Hand in Takt 15 in die Nähe des D, bevor du das vorangehende Gis spielst. S. 38

### Bedrich Smetana
*Andante in F Minor* (Andante in f-Moll). [♩ = 50–56] Dieses kurze Albumblatt stammt aus dem Jahre 1880. In diesem Werk muss man sich besonders um die linke Hand kümmern, so dass die melodische Linie klar herausgehört werden kann. Smetanas Klaviermusik schließt viele einzelne, kurze Charakterstücke mit ein. Von diesen ist das vorliegende wahrscheinlich das kürzeste. Die Pedalbezeichnungen sind vom Komponisten selbst. S. 34

### Sergej Bortkiewicz
*Through the Desert* (Durch die Wüste). [♩ = 102–108] Bortkiewiczs ,The Little Wanderer', aus dem dieses Stück entnommen ist, wurde 1923 erstmals veröffentlicht und ist zweifellos das Ergebnis seiner Arbeit als Lehrer. In dieser Sammlung portraitiert Bortkiewicz sowohl unterschiedliche Aspekte des Reisens als auch die Länder, die der kleine Wanderer besucht. Dieses Stück ist ein wunderbar geschriebenes, zweistimmiges Werk, das dabei hilft, diesen Aspekt des Stimmen-Spielens zu fördern. S. 34

### Frédéric Chopin
*Bourrée.* [♩ = 120–128] Dieses Stück, das erstmals im Jahre 1968 bei Schott veröffentlicht und von Ates Orga herausgegeben wurde, ist des Komponisten Harmonisierung einer volkstümlichen Melodie. Chopin beabsichtigte nicht, es zu veröffentlichen, wie die fehlende Artikulation und Dynamik anzudeuten scheint. Genau dieser Umstand macht es für pädagogische Zwecke so interessant, da es Raum für Experimente und Entscheidungen lässt, die sowohl den Schüler als auch den Lehrer beteiligen. Spieler mit kleineren Händen müssen vielleicht die Akkorde der linken Hand in den Takten 11 und 15 neu einrichten. Oktaven können gebrochen werden, aber der letzte Akkord in Takt 15 muss wahrscheinlich ohne das D gespielt werden, während das Cis eine Oktave tiefer gespielt wird. S. 35

**Peter Tschaikowsky**

Beide Stücke von Tschaikowsky sind einer Sammlung von 24 Stücken mit dem Titel *Children's Album, op. 39* (Kinderalbum, op. 39) entnommen. Tschaikowskys Untertitel *Collection of easy pieces for children à la Schumann* (Eine Sammlung einfacher Stücke für Kinder à la Schumann) macht klar, dass Schumanns *Album für die Jugend* ihn zu seinem Werk inspirierte.

*The Doll's Illness* (Die kranke Puppe). [♩ = 50–54] Ganz zu Beginn kann es nützlich sein, beide Hände getrennt zu üben, aber einen genauen Eindruck des Stückes bekommt man nur, wenn man mit beiden Händen gleichzeitig übt. Abhängig von dem Gesamtklang, den man erzeugen will, kann die Melodielinie entweder über die anderen Stimmen dominieren oder sie kann Teil der Gesamtstruktur sein. Der Gebrauch des rechten Pedals wird nicht vorgeschrieben, ist aber fast unabdingbar ein wichtiger Teil des Stückes.                                            S. 37

*The New Doll* (Die neue Puppe). [♩. = 96–104] Dieses Musikstück wird ganz klar von der rechten Hand geführt. Passe die Begleitung der linken Hand so an, dass die melodische Linie in der rechten unterstützt wird.                                            S. 42

**Robert Volkmann**

Beide Musikstücke von Volkmann sind Teil einer Sammlung mit 13 Stücken, genannt *Grandmother's Songs, op. 27* (Großmutters Lieder, op. 27), die erstmals bei Schott veröffentlicht wurden.

*Op. 27 No. 3* [♩ = 84–88] ist ein ausdrucksstarkes Miniaturstück, das einem die Gelegenheit bietet, langsames Legato zu üben.                                            S. 39

*Op. 27 No. 11* [♩. = 76–80] ist ein Showstück, das eine hohe Geschicklichkeit der linken Hand und eine eindeutige Koordinationsfähigkeit zwischen beiden Händen erfordert, besonders in den Takten 20 bis 33.                                            S. 46

**Michail Glinka**

*Polka.* [♩ = 100–104] Ein gemäßigt lebhaftes Stück, bei dem man auf verschiedene Aspekte hören sollte. Mache erstens einen Unterschied zwischen der Legato- und Staccato-Artikulation in Takt 3 sowie dem Legato-Bogen in Takt 7. Spiele zweitens die linke Hand im ganzen Stück gestoßen. Das ergibt einen schönen Kontrast zur rechten Hand, die hauptsächlich Legato gespielt wird. Und drittens kannst du in Takt 3 den Daumen der linken Hand gleichzeitig für G und A benutzen, wenn du ihn etwas seitlich stellst.                                            S. 40

**Nicolaj Rimskij-Korsakow**

*Allegretto.* [♩ = 92–98] Die äußeren Teile dieses Stückes helfen, die Fähigkeiten zum zweistimmigen Spiel weiterzuentwickeln, die uns zum ersten Mal in Bortkiewiczs *Through the Desert* (S. 34) begegneten. Der Mittelteil von Takt 33 bis 48 enthält zwei Takte mit Oktaven, die mit beiden Händen gespielt werden können, wenn das Gesamttempo dabei beibehalten wird.                                            S. 41

**Sergej Ljapunow**

*Invention.* [♩ = 84–92] Nach den Stücken von Bortkiewicz und Rimskij-Korsakow (S. 34, 40) ist dieses eine weitere Möglichkeit, das mehrstimmige Spielen zu entwickeln, aber diesmal in einer schwierigeren Tonart. Folge in den Takten 9 bis 14 den Phrasierungsbögen jeder Linie, um diese Sequenz in kleineren Einheiten von ein bis eineinhalb Takten zu lernen. Was die Dynamik betrifft, bewegt sich die Musik nur zwischen *mf* und *p*.                                            S. 44

# Biographical notes

**Cornelius Gurlitt** (1820–1901). Born and worked in Hamburg, Germany. He was particularly successful as a composer of educational music, most of it for piano. Among his works are also some chamber music and a *Symphony for piano and children's instruments op. 169* (meaning for piano and orchestral instruments for young players). Stylistically, some of his works were influenced by Schumann.

**Félix Le Couppey** (1811–1887) was a professor of piano at the Paris Conservatoire. Nowadays he is best remembered for his influential piano pegagogical works which include *L'ABC du Piano* and *24 Études primaries*. Le Couppey wrote a significant amount of music for beginners, most of which displays his gift for melody.

**Fritz Spindler** (1817–1905) lived and worked in Dresden, Germany. He was a prolific composer who was known for writing in an easily accessible style. Among his many educational works is the *Kindersymphony op. 390* (using orchestral instruments but writing for young players). Spindler also wrote some non-educational works, including a piano concerto and some chamber music.

**Robert Schumann** (1810–1856) was one of the 19th century's most significant composers. He was also an active writer on musical topics and as such was influential in promoting music by other composers, most notably the young Brahms. Until 1839 Schumann wrote almost exclusively piano music before branching out into chamber music, songs and orchestral works. His stylistic influence can be felt in a number of 19th-century composers.

**Carl Reinecke** (1824–1910) was born in Hamburg, Germany, but worked in Leipzig where he had considerable influence on musical life. An editor, composer, conductor, pianist and teacher, Reinecke was a well established and respected musician. His large output includes much chamber music which was popular in its day. Nowadays he is mostly remembered for his educational music, particularly for piano.

**Vincent d'Indy** (1851–1931). Born and worked in Paris. He studied composition with César Franck whose ideas influenced him greatly. D'Indy's reputation is based on his chamber music, orchestral works and the *Symphony on a French mountain song* for piano and orchestra (1886).

**Johann Friedrich Burgmüller** (1806–1874) was born in Regensburg, Germany. From 1832 onwards he lived in Paris, where he worked as a piano teacher and composer of educational music. His *Études* opp. 73, 100 and 105 have long been an established part of the piano repertoire for students.

**Robert Fuchs** (1847–1927) worked as a professor of piano at the Conservatoire in Vienna. A versatile composer of orchestral, chamber, vocal and piano music, Fuchs is best remembered today for his serenades for orchestra. His piano music contains many educational titles, including études, preludes and character pieces.

**Charles Gounod** (1818–1893). French composer of opera, instrumental and vocal music. His first major success, the opera *Faust* (1859) established him as a composer who was to have a significant influence on the next generation of French composers, including Bizet, Fauré and Massenet. Gounod wrote only a small number of works for piano.

**Bedrich Smetana** (1824–1884) was a Czech pianist, conductor and composer who worked in Prague and Goeteburg. Works such as the opera *The Bartered Bride* (1866/70) and the symphonic poem *Má vlast* ('my fatherland') ensured his reputation as the first major nationalist composer in Bohemia. His piano music is influenced by two major factors: his use of folk material (in polkas and furiants) and the pianism of Liszt, which inspired Smetana's most demanding piano work, the concert study *At the seashore*.

**Sergei Bortkiewicz** (1877–1952). Ukranian-born, he spent the majority of his life working as a pianist and piano teacher in Austria and Germany. Bortkiewicz studied composition with Lyadov at the St Petersburg conservatoire (1896–99) and subsequently piano with Reisenauer and composition with Jadassohn at the Leipzig Conservatoire. Musically, Bortkiewicz's style is influenced by Chopin, Liszt and early Rachmaninov.

**Frédéric Chopin** (1810–1849). Polish composer. Chopin was one of the most influential 19th-century composers. Applying himself predominantly to the writing of piano music, Chopin's contribution to the development of piano technique was considerable. Harmonically, he influenced, amongst others, such diverse composers as Liszt and Fauré, Debussy and Rachmaninov. Chopin can be credited with establishing the *ballade* as a piano piece and popularizing the *mazurka* in the 19th century.

**Peter Tchaikovsky** (1840–1893). Russian composer. Tchaikovsky's piano music consists of over a hundred pieces, including the large scale *Grand Sonata* op. 37 and pieces for beginners in the *Children's Album* op. 39. Tchaikovsky was a major influence on Russian and international musical life. His works include symphonic music, ballets, vocal and chamber music.

**Robert Volkmann** (1815–1883). Born in Germany, Volkmann worked in Prague and Pest (Hungary). At the time, his most successful works were the symphonic pieces, including a cello concerto. Today, Volkmann is remembered mostly for his chamber music, particularly the two piano trios opp. 3 and 5. His piano music consists of a number of smaller character pieces and some concert repertoire.

**Mikhail Glinka** (1804–1857) has often been called the 'father of Russian music'. Glinka's opera 'A life for the Tsar' (1836) established him as Russia's leading composer of his time. Among his piano music are variations on operatic melodies and a number of character pieces. Glinka's music influenced a substantial number of younger Russian composers, most notably Balakirev, Rimsky-Korsakov and Musorgsky.

**Nicolai Rimsky-Korsakov** (1844–1908) initially trained as a naval officer before studying composition. He held a series of musical posts in his native Russia, where he became a sought-after teacher of harmony and composition. Among his students were Glazunov, Lyadov, Prokofiev and Stravinsky. Rimsky-Korsakov's works include operas, orchestral works, (including Sheherazade of 1888), a piano concerto and a relatively small number of piano pieces.

**Sergey Lyapunov** (1859–1924) was a Russian composer, pianist and conductor. Stylistically influenced by the nationalism of Balakirev and the pianism of Liszt, he developed a virtuoso approach to writing piano music. Much of his music draws on the use of folk material which he fuses with the above influences to create a distinct style of his own.

Bibliography:

Hinson, Maurice, *Guide to the Pianist's Repertoire*, Bloomington and Indianapolis, Indiana University Press, 2000.
Prosnitz, Adolf, *Handbuch der Klavierliteratur*, Vienna, Doblinger, 1908.
Ruthardt, Adolf, *Wegweiser durch die Klavierliteratur*, Leipzig and Zürich, Gebrüder Hug & Co., 1910.
Sadie, Stanley (ed.), *Grove Concise Dictonary of Music*, London, Macmillan Publishers Ltd, 1988.

Nils Franke

## Notes biographiques

**Cornelius Gurlitt** (1820–1901). Natif de Hambourg en Allemagne, c'est dans cette ville qu'il travailla toute sa vie. Il connut un grand succès en tant que compositeur de musique à vocation pédagogique, le plus souvent pour le piano. Parmi ses œuvres figurent également quelques pièces de musique de chambre et une *Symphonie pour piano et instruments d'enfants* op. 169 (c'est-à-dire pour piano et orchestre de jeunes instrumentistes). D'un point de vue stylistique, certaines de ses œuvres révèlent l'influence de Schumann.

**Félix Le Couppey** (1811–1887) était professeur de piano au conservatoire de Paris. Actuellement, sa réputation se fonde sur ses importantes œuvres pédagogiques pour piano qui comprennent *L'ABC du Piano* et les *24 Études primaires*. Le Couppey a écrit un nombre significatif de pièces pour débutants qui illustrent pour la plupart son don pour la mélodie.

**Fritz Spindler** (1817–1905) vivait et travaillait à Dresde, en Allemagne. C'était un compositeur prolifique réputé pour son style facilement accessible. Parmi ses nombreuses œuvres pédagogiques compte la *Kindersymphony* op. 390 (qui utilise des instruments symphoniques, mais est écrite pour jeunes instrumentistes). Spindler a également écrit des œuvres de répertoire, notamment un concerto pour piano et de la musique de chambre.

**Robert Schumann** (1810–1856) est l'un des compositeurs les plus marquants du 19e siècle. Il est également l'auteur de nombreux écrits sur la musique et a largement influé sur la diffusion de la musique d'autres compositeurs, dont notamment le jeune Brahms. Jusqu'en 1839, Schumann a écrit presque exclusivement de la musique pour piano avant de se lancer dans la musique de chambre, le chant et le répertoire orchestral. Son influence stylistique est sensible dans l'œuvre de nombreux autres compositeurs du 19e siècle.

**Carl Reinecke** (1824–1910) est né en Allemagne, à Hambourg, mais travaillait à Leipzig où son influence sur la vie musicale fut très importante. À la fois éditeur, compositeur, chef d'orchestre, pianiste et professeur, Reinecke était un musicien établi et respecté. Sa grande production comprend beaucoup de musique de chambre très populaire à l'époque. Il est maintenant surtout reconnu pour ses œuvres pédagogiques, notamment pour le piano.

**Vincent d'Indy** (1851–1931). Natif de Paris où il exerça également ses activités, Vincent d'Indy étudia la composition avec César Franck qui eut une grande influence sur lui. Sa réputation est fondée essentiellement sur sa musique de chambre, ses œuvres orchestrales et sa *Symphonie sur un chant montagnard français* pour piano et orchestre (1886).

**Johann Friedrich Burgmüller** (1806–1874) est né en Allemagne, à Regensbourg. À partir de 1832, il vécut à Paris où il travailla en tant que professeur de piano et compositeur de répertoire pédagogique. Ses études op. 73, 100 et 105 ont figuré pendant longtemps au répertoire des élèves pianistes.

**Robert Fuchs** (1847–1927) était professeur de piano au conservatoire de Vienne. Compositeur aux dons multiples, il se consacra aussi bien à la musique orchestrale, à la musique de chambre et à la musique chorale qu'au répertoire pour piano. Actuellement, ses sérénades pour piano sont les plus connues. Son œuvre pour piano comprend de nombreuses pièces pédagogiques, études, préludes et pièces de caractère.

**Charles Gounod** (1818–1893). Compositeur français d'opéras, de musique instrumentale et vocale. Son premier succès majeur, *Faust* (1859), lui conféra le rayonnement qui allait influencer largement la génération suivante de compositeurs et notamment Bizet, Fauré et Massenet. Gounod n'a écrit que très peu pour le piano.

**Bedrich Smetana** (1824–1884) était un pianiste, chef d'orchestre et compositeur tchèque qui travailla à Prague et Göteborg. Sa réputation de premier compositeur nationaliste de Bohême fut assurée par des œuvres telles que son opéra *The Bartered Bride* (1866/70) et le poème symphonique *Má vlast* (ma patrie). Sa musique pour piano est influencée par deux facteurs majeurs : l'utilisation de matériaux empruntés à la musique folklorique (dans les polkas et les furiants) et l'art pianistique de Liszt qui a inspiré à Smetana son œuvre pour piano la plus exigeante, l'étude de concert *Au bord de la mer*.

**Sergei Bortkiewicz** (1877–1952). Né en Ukraine, il exerça la majeure partie de sa vie le métier de pianiste et de professeur de piano, en Autriche et en Allemagne. Bortkiewicz a étudié la composition avec Lyadov au conservatoire de Saint-Pétersbourg (1896–99) et, par la suite, le piano avec Reisenauer et la composition avec Jadassohn au conservatoire de Leipzig. Musicalement, le style de Bortkiewicz est marqué par Chopin, Liszt et par les premières œuvres de Rachmaninov.

**Frédéric Chopin** (1810–1849). D'origine polonaise, Chopin fut l'un des compositeurs les plus influents du 19e siècle. Il se consacra principalement à l'écriture pour le piano, et sa contribution au développement de la technique pianistique fut considérable. Sur le plan harmonique, son influence est sensible sur des compositeurs aussi variés que Liszt et Fauré, Debussy et Rachmaninov, pour n'en citer que quelques uns. On doit également à Chopin l'entrée de la *ballade* dans le répertoire pour piano et la popularisation de la *mazurka* au 19e siècle.

**Piotr Tchaïkovski** (1840–1893). Compositeur russe. Sa musique pour piano comprend plus de cent œuvres, parmi lesquelles la *Grand Sonata* op. 37, œuvre de grande envergure, et des pièces pour débutants dans l'*Album pour les enfants* op. 39. Tchaïkovski a exercé une influence majeure sur la vie musicale russe et internationale. Ses œuvres englobent également de la musique symphonique, de la musique de ballets, de la musique vocale et de la musique de chambre.

**Robert Volkmann** (1815–1883). Né en Allemagne, Volkmann a travaillé à Prague et à Pest (Hongrie). À l'époque, ses œuvres les plus célèbres étaient ses œuvres symphoniques, dont un concerto pour violoncelle. À l'heure actuelle, Volkmann est surtout connu pour sa musique de chambre, en particulier les deux trios avec piano op. 3 et 5. Sa musique pour piano est composée de nombreuses petites pièces de caractère et de quelques pièces de concert.

**Mikhail Glinka** (1804–1857) a souvent été surnommé le "père de la musique russe". Son opéra, *La vie d'un Tsar* (1836), a fait de lui le compositeur phare de la Russie en son temps. Parmi ses œuvres pour piano, on compte des variations sur des airs d'opéra ainsi que de nombreuses pièces de caractère. La musique de Glinka a influencé le travail de nombreux jeunes compositeurs russes dont les plus notables sont Balakirev, Rimski-Korsakov et Moussorgski.

**Nicolaï Rimski-Korsakov** (1844–1908). Reçut une formation initiale d'officier de marine avant d'étudier la composition. Il occupa ensuite une série de postes liés à la musique dans sa Russie natale où il devint un professeur d'harmonie et de composition très recherché. Parmi ses étudiants figuraient Glazunov, Lyadov, Prokofiev et Stravinsky. L'œuvre de Rimski-Korsakov comprend des opéras, des œuvres orchestrales (y compris *Shéhérazade* –1888), un concerto pour piano et un nombre relativement réduit de pièces pour piano.

**Sergey Lyapunov** (1859–1924) était un compositeur, pianiste et chef d'orchestre russe. Son style était influencé par le nationalisme de Balakirev et le style de Liszt, et il développa une approche virtuose de l'écriture pianistique. Nombreuses sont ses œuvres illustrant l'utilisation de matériaux issus du folklore qu'il fusionne avec les autres influences citées afin de créer un style distinct de son invention.

Bibliographie :

Hinson, Maurice, *Guide to the Pianist's Repertoire*, Bloomington et Indianapolis, Indiana University Press, 2000.
Prosnitz, Adolf, *Handbuch der Klavierliteratur*, Vienne, Doblinger, 1908.
Ruthardt, Adolf, *Wegweiser durch die Klavierliteratur*, Leipzig et Zürich, Gebrüder Hug & Co., 1910.
Sadie, Stanley (éd.), *Grove Concise Dictionary of Music*, Londres, Macmillan Publishers Ltd, 1988.

Nils Franke

# Biografische Anmerkungen

**Cornelius Gurlitt** (1820–1901) wurde in Hamburg geboren und arbeitete auch dort. Er war besonders als Komponist von Musiklehrwerken erfolgreich, vor allem für das Klavier. Zu seinen Werken gehören auch Kammermusik und eine *Symphonie für Klavier und Kinderinstrumente op. 169* (d. h. für Klavier und Orchesterinstrumente für junge Spieler). Einige seiner Werke wurden stilistisch von Schumann beeinflusst.

**Félix Le Couppey** (1811–1887) war Professor für Klavier am Pariser Konservatorium. Heutzutage erinnert man sich hauptsächlich wegen seiner einflussreichen pädagogischen Klavierwerke an ihn, die *L'ABC du Piano* und *24 Études primaries* miteinschließen. Le Couppey schrieb eine beachtliche Anzahl von Stücken für Anfänger, von denen die meisten seine Begabung für Melodien widerspiegeln.

**Fritz Spindler** (1817–1905) lebte und arbeitete in Dresden. Er war ein produktiver Komponist, der für seinen einfach zugänglichen Stil bekannt war. Zu seinen vielen Lehrwerken gehört die *Kindersymphonie op. 390* (er verwendet Orchesterinstrumente, schreibt aber für junge Spieler). Spindler schrieb auch einige Werke ohne pädagogischen Hintergrund, unter anderem ein Klavierkonzert und einige Kammermusikstücke.

**Robert Schumann** (1810–1856) war einer der bedeutendsten Komponisten des 19. Jahrhunderts. Außerdem verfasste er viele Artikel zu musikalischen Themen und war daher für die Verbreitung von Musik anderer Komponisten, insbesondere die des jungen Brahms, bedeutsam. Bis 1839 schrieb Schumann fast ausschließlich Klaviermusik bevor er sich auch mit Kammermusik, Liedern und Orchesterwerken befasste. Seinen stilistischen Einfluss erkennt man bei einer Anzahl von Komponisten des 19. Jahrhunderts wieder.

**Carl Reinecke** (1824–1910) wurde in Hamburg geboren, arbeitete aber in Leipzig, wo er einen beträchtlichen Einfluss auf das musikalische Leben ausübte. Als Herausgeber, Komponist, Dirigent, Pianist und Lehrer war Reinecke ein sehr angesehener und geachteter Musiker. Sein umfangreiches Schaffen umfasst viel Kammermusik, die damals sehr beliebt war. Heutzutage erinnert man sich hauptsächlich wegen seiner Lehrwerke an ihn, insbesondere der für Klavier.

**Vincent d'Indy** (1851–1931) wurde in Paris geboren und arbeitete auch dort. Er studierte Komposition bei César Franck, dessen Ideen ihn stark beeinflussten. D'Indys Ansehen begründet sich auf seine Kammermusik, seine Orchesterwerke und die *Symphony on a French mountain song* (Sinfonie über ein französisches Gebirgslied) für Klavier und Orchester (1886).

**Johann Friedrich Burgmüller** (1806–1874) wurde in Regensburg geboren. Ab 1832 lebte er in Paris, wo er als Klavierlehrer und Komponist von Musiklehrwerken arbeitete. Seine *Études* op. 73, 100, 105 sind schon lange für jeden Schüler ein fester Bestandteil des Klavierrepertoires.

**Robert Fuchs** (1847–1927) arbeitete als Professor für Klavier am Wiener Konservatorium. Als vielseitiger Komponist von Orchester-, Kammer-, Vokal- und Klaviermusik ist er heutzutage hauptsächlich wegen seiner Orchesterserenaden in Erinnerung. Seine Klaviermusik enthält viele Lehrtitel, die Etüden, Präludien und Charakterstücke miteinschließen.

**Charles Gounod** (1818–1893) war ein französischer Komponist von Opern, Instrumental- und Vokalmusik. Sein erster größerer Erfolg, die Oper *Faust* (1859), etablierte ihn als einen Komponisten, der einen bedeutenden Einfluss auf die nächste Generation französischer Komponisten ausüben sollte, darunter Bizet, Fauré und Massenet. Gounod schrieb nur wenige Werke für Klavier.

**Bedrich Smetana** (1824–1884) war ein tschechischer Pianist, Dirigent und Komponist, der in Prag und Göteborg arbeitete. Werke wie die Oper *Die verkaufte Braut* (1866/70) und die symphonische Dichtung *Má vlast* (Mein Vaterland) sicherten ihm seinen Ruf als Hauptvertreter der Nationalen Schule in Böhmen. Seine Klaviermusik ist durch zwei Hauptfaktoren gekennzeichnet: Dem Gebrauch von volkstümlichem Material (in Polkas und Furianten) und Liszts Klavierspiel, das Smetana zu seinem anspruchsvollsten Klavierwerk inspirierte, der Konzertetüde *Am Meeresgestade*.

**Sergej Bortkiewicz** (1877–1952) wurde in der Ukraine geboren und verbrachte den größten Teil seines Lebens in Österreich und Deutschland, wo er als Pianist und Klavierlehrer arbeitete. Bortkiewicz studierte Komposition bei Ljadow am Konservatorium in St. Petersburg (1896–99) und danach Klavier bei Reisenauer und Komposition bei Jadassohn am Leipziger Konservatorium. Musikalisch wird Bortkiewieczs Stil von Chopin, Liszt und dem frühen Rachmaninov beeinflusst.

**Frédéric Chopin** (1810–1849) was ein polnischer Komponist. Er war einer der einflussreichsten Komponisten des 19. Jahrhunderts. Indem er sich hauptsächlich dem Schreiben von Klaviermusik widmete, trug Chopin maßgeblich zur Entwicklung der Klaviertechnik bei. In harmonischer Hinsicht beeinflusste er unter anderen so unterschiedliche Komponisten wie Liszt und Fauré, Debussy und Rachmaninow. Es ist Chopins Verdienst, die *Ballade* als Klavierstück zu etablieren und das Ansehen der *Mazurka* im 19. Jahrhundert stark anzuheben.

**Peter Tschaikowsky** (1840–1893) war ein russischer Komponist. Tschaikowskys Klaviermusik besteht aus über 100 Stücken, einschließlich der umfangreichen *Großen Sonate op. 37* und Anfängerstücken im *Kinderalbum op. 39*. Tschaikowsky nahm großen Einfluss auf das russische und internationale musikalische Leben. Seine Werke schließen symphonische Musik, Ballette, Vokal- und Kammermusik mit ein.

**Robert Volkmann** (1815–1883) wurde in Deutschland geboren und arbeitete in Prag und Pest (Ungarn). Zur damaligen Zeit waren seine erfolgreichsten Werke die symphonischen Stücke, einschließlich eines Cellokonzertes. Heutzutage erinnert man sich an Volkmann hauptsächlich wegen seiner Kammermusik, besonders den beiden Klaviertrios op. 3 und 5. Seine Klaviermusik besteht aus einer Anzahl kleiner Charakterstücke und Konzertrepertoire.

**Michail Glinka** (1804–1857) wurde oft der ‚Vater der russischen Musik' genannt. Glinkas Oper *Das Leben für den Zaren* (1836) etablierte ihn als den führenden russischen Komponisten

seiner Zeit. Zu seiner Klaviermusik gehören Variationen über Opernmelodien und eine Anzahl von Charakterstücken. Glinkas Musik beeinflusste eine beträchtliche Zahl jüngerer russischer Komponisten, vor allem Balakirew, Rimskij-Korsakow und Mussorgskij.

**Nicolaj Rimskij-Korsakow** (1844–1908) ließ sich ursprünglich zum Marineoffizier ausbilden, bevor er Komposition studierte. Er hatte eine Reihe von musikalischen Positionen in seinem heimatlichen Russland inne, wo er ein begehrter Lehrer für Harmonielehre und Komposition wurde. Zu seinen Schülern gehören Glasunow, Ljadow, Prokofjew und Strawinsky. Rimskij-Korsakows Werke umfassen Opern, Orchesterwerke (einschließlich *Scheherazade* (1888)), ein Klavierkonzert und eine relativ kleine Anzahl von Klavierstücken.

**Sergej Ljapunow** (1859–1924) war ein russischer Komponist, Pianist und Dirigent. Stilistisch wurde er von Balakirevs Nationalismus und Liszts Klavierspiel beeinflusst und entwickelte so eine virtuose Herangehensweise an das Schreiben von Klaviermusik. Ein großer Teil seiner Musik stützt sich auf volkstümliches Material, das er mit den oben genannten Einflüssen vermischt, um einen ganz eigenen Stil zu entwickeln.

Bibliografie:

Hinson, Maurice, *Guide to the Pianist's Repertoire*, Bloomington und Indianapolis, Indiana University Press, 2000.
Prosnitz, Adolf, *Handbuch der Klavierliteratur*, Wien, Doblinger, 1908.
Ruthardt, Adolf, *Wegweiser durch die Klavierliteratur*, Leipzig und Zürich, Gebrüder Hug & Co., 1910.
Sadie, Stanley (hrsg.), *Grove Concise Dictonary of Music*, London, Macmillan Publishers Ltd, 1988.

Nils Franke

# Grading Repertoire

## International Grading Systems

Grading repertoire is an essential tool in instrumental and vocal pedagogy. Presenting music in a progressive order is an approach to teaching that can be found in tutor and repertoire books across the world and throughout the ages. Whilst many resources agree on this basic format, the labelling and identifying of different stages of musical development have proved more elusive. Some countries measure instrumental and vocal progress by a succession of grades, whilst others have levels or steps. A pianistic development from the first piece in this book, Gurlitt's *Allegretto grazioso*, to some of the most challenging works in the piano repertoire can embrace anything from six to 11 identifiable levels, grades or steps, depending on the system used. In the Anglo/American world, as well as the Far East, external examination boards provide a graded approach through a number of progressive syllabi. In many European countries, youth music organisations (sometimes attached to regional conservatoires or youth music competitions) may set syllabus requirements or publish sample repertoire lists.

Given the diversity of international approaches to the grading and labelling of pedagogical repertoire, it is not surprising that no system can cater for all countries. As such, it is probably more appropriate to suggest that a student starting to use this book should have between 2–3 years' playing experience. In terms of levels, steps or grades, this would be Grade 1 (UK and Commonwealth), late beginner or elementary (USA) or early level 1 (Germany).

## Criteria for the Selection of Repertoire

It can often be a challenging task to select music for a student that is appropriate for his/her stage of development, yet appeals to the student purely on a musical level. The criteria for selection are thus a mixture of the following points:
• Technical/musical requirements of the piece
• Technical/musical ability of the student
• Notational skills
• Physical aspects (such as size of hand, ability to reach pedals)
• Age category of student: a younger student, a teenage learner or an adult student.

## The Graded Repertoire in this Anthology

Applying these criteria has led to the inclusion of a broad range of repertoire at this level, aimed at the different categories of students identified above. All metronome markings are editorial and are intended to be suggestions only. Some works, such as the pieces by Chopin, Smetana and Rimsky-Korsakov, require a larger hand span and are therefore aimed at those students who can stretch an octave comfortably. The use of the right pedal is a skill that students can develop in a number of pieces in this book. Tchaikovsky's *The Doll's Illness* is particularly useful in this respect. This selection of 30 pieces is intended to present a wide range of styles and combine established teaching repertoire with lesser-known works. It also aims to juxtapose easier pieces with some that contain musical, notational and technical challenges!

Nils Franke

# 1. Allegretto Grazioso

Cornelius Gurlitt

# 2. Mélodie (Melody)

Félix Le Couppey

# 3. Song without Words

Fritz Spindler

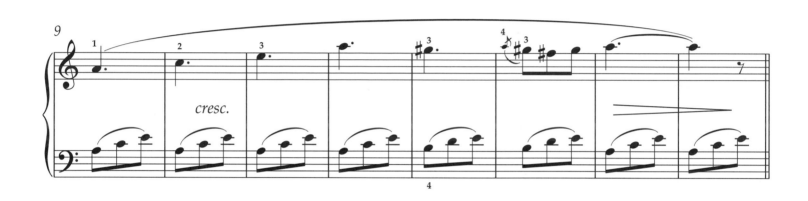

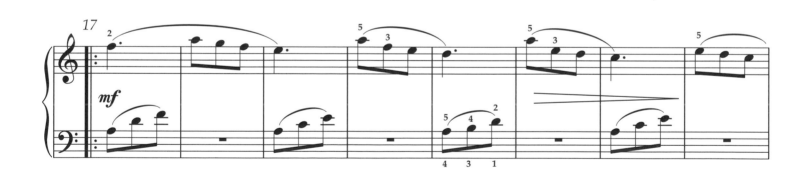

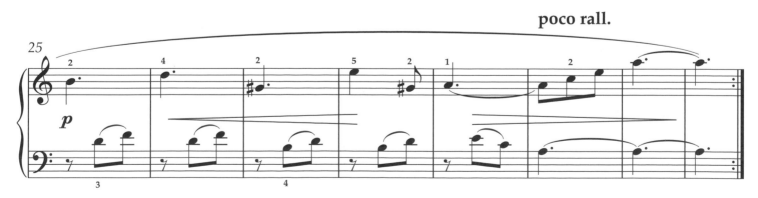

# 4. Air arabe (Arabian Air)
## Melody

Félix Le Couppey

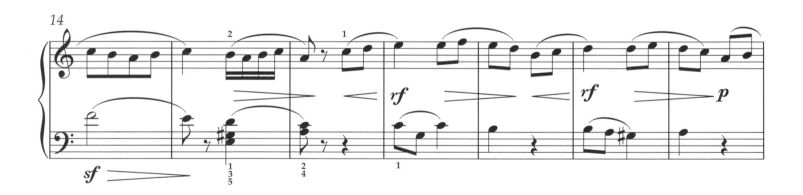

from • de • aus: ED 8946

# 5. Bärentanz (Bear Dance)

Robert Schumann

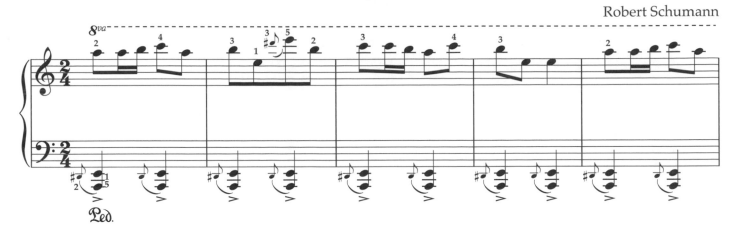

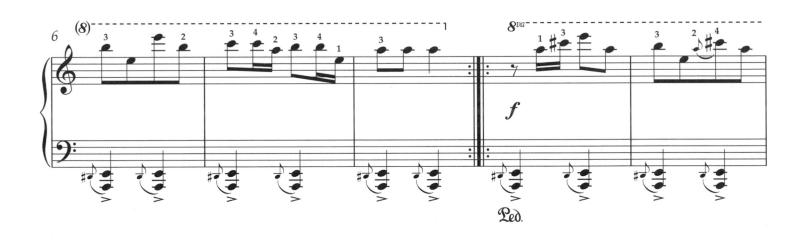

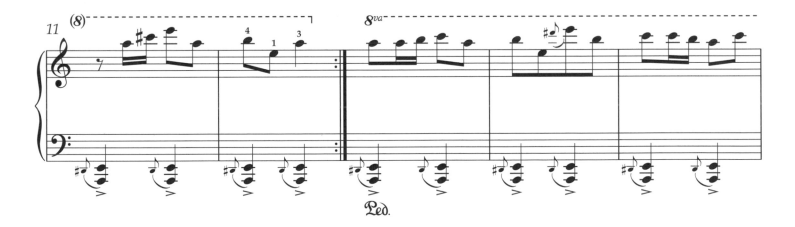

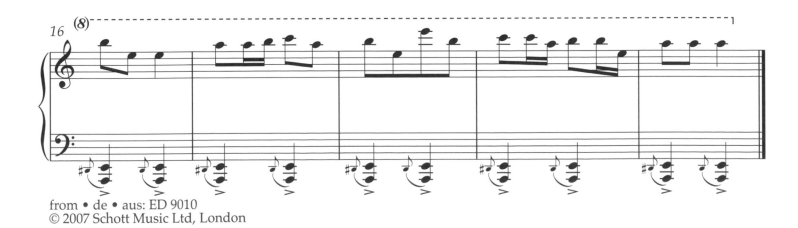

from • de • aus: ED 9010
© 2007 Schott Music Ltd, London

# 6. Prelude

Carl Reinecke

# 7. Stückchen (Little Piece)

Robert Schumann

**Nicht schnell***

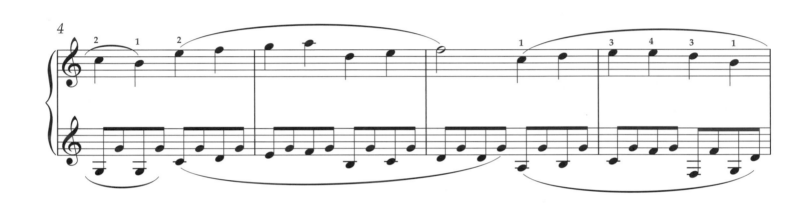

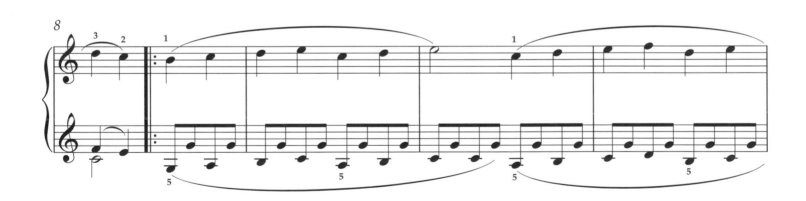

from • de • aus: ED 9010
© 2007 Schott Music Ltd, London

*non presto • not fast • pas vite

# 8. Gavotte

Cornelius Gurlitt

**Moderato**

from • de • aus: ED 196

# 9. Petite pièce (Little Piece)

Vincent d'Indy

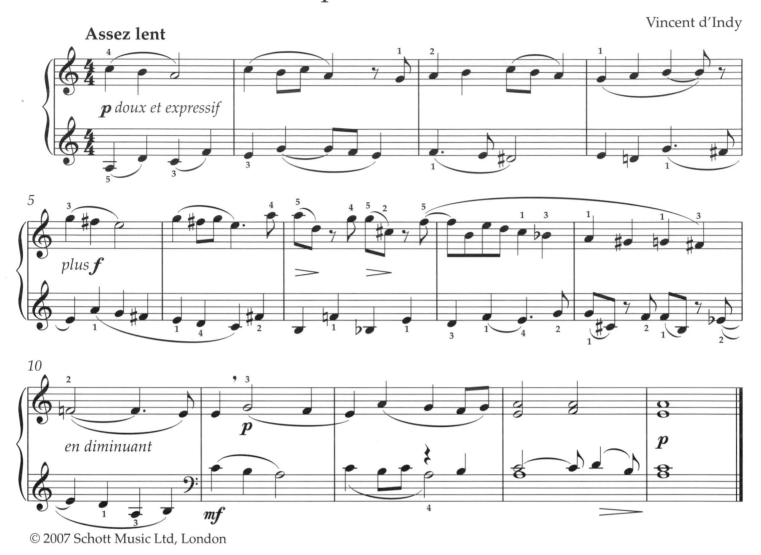

# 10. Melodie (Melody)

Robert Schumann

from • de • aus: ED 9010

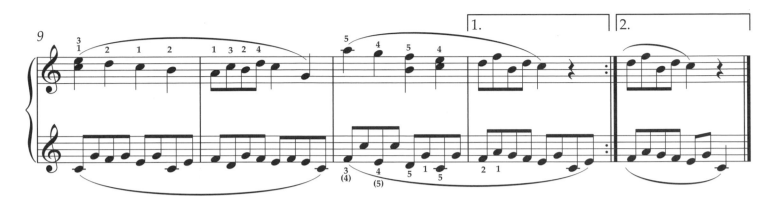

## 11. Soldatenmarsch (Soldiers' March)

Robert Schumann

**Munter und straff\***

from • de • aus: ED 9010
© 2007 Schott Music Ltd, London

\*Arzillo e teso • brisk, taut • allègrement et tiré

# 12. Arabesque

Johann Burgmüller

from • de • aus: ED 173

# 13. Allegro non Troppo

Cornelius Gurlitt

# 14. Les Pifferari (The Bagpipers)

## Impromptu

Charles Gounod

# 15. Stolzer Reitersmann (Proud Horseman)

Robert Fuchs

# 16. Étude No. 17

Félix Le Couppey

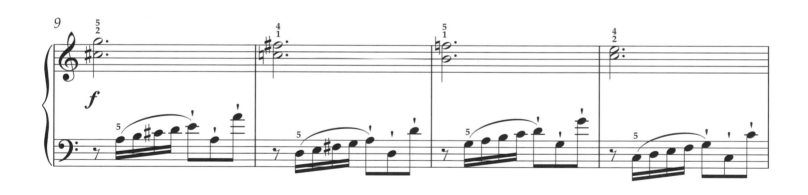

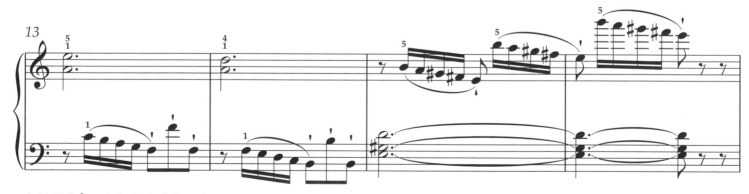

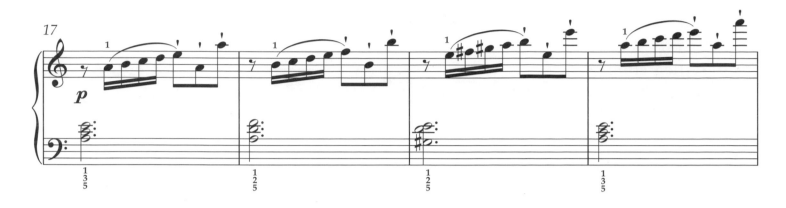

## 17. Étude No. 15

Félix Le Couppey

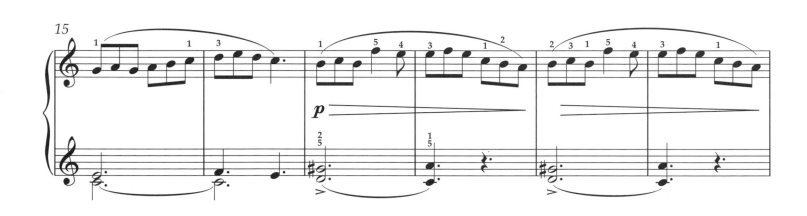

*D.C. al Fine*

# 18. Andante in F Minor

Bedřich Smetana

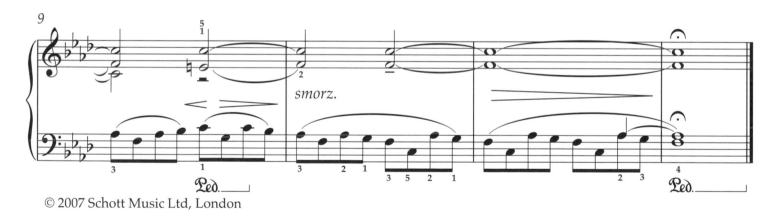

# 19. Through the Desert

Sergei Bortkiewicz

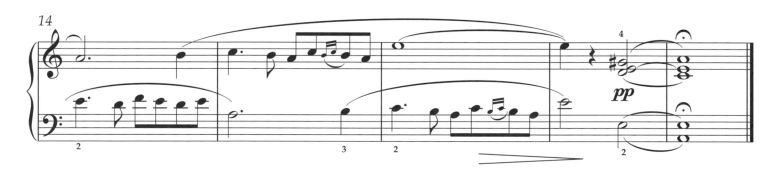

# 20. Bourrée

Frédéric Chopin

from • de • aus: ED 10984

# 21. Haschemann

Robert Schumann

**So schnell als möglich***

from • de • aus: ED 9010

*più presto possibile • as fast as possible • le plus vite possible

## 22. The Doll's Illness

Peter Tchaikovsky

from • de • aus: ED 4748

## 23. Banges Herzelein (Sad at Heart)

Robert Fuchs

# 24. Op. 27 No. 3

Robert Volkmann

**Ziemlich langsam**

# 25. Polka

Mikhail Glinka

# 26. Allegretto

Nicolai Rimsky-Korsakov

# 27. The New Doll

Peter Tchaikovsky

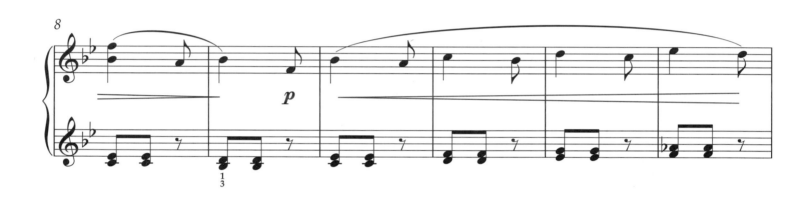

from • de • aus: ED 4748

# 28. Invention

Sergey Lyapunov

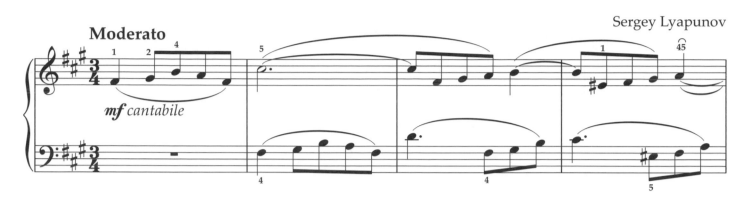

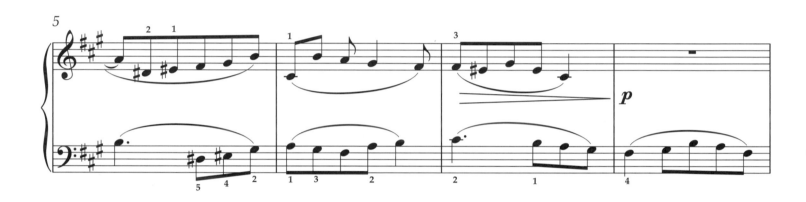

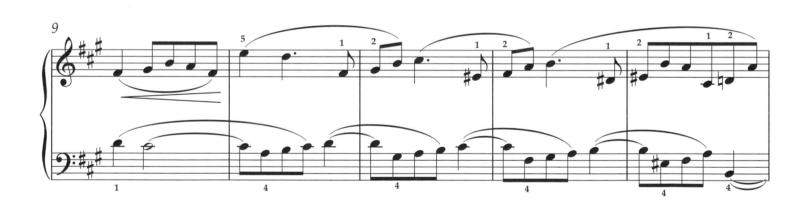

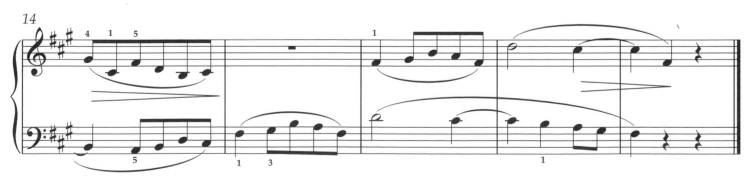

# 29. Kuckuck im Versteck (Cuckoo in Hiding)

Robert Schumann

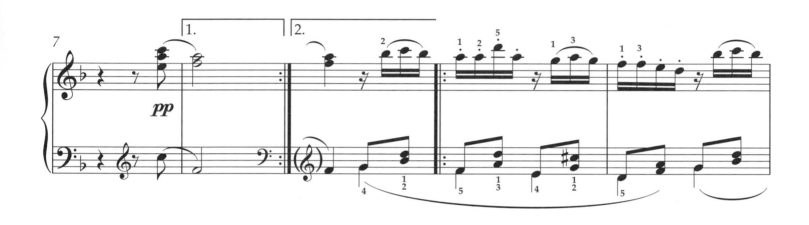

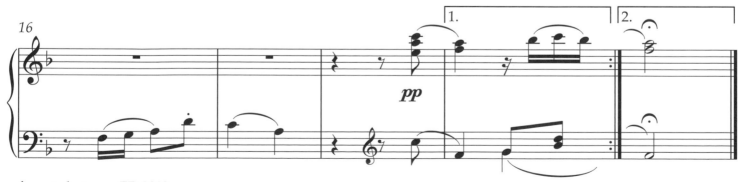

from • de • aus: ED 9010
© 2007 Schott Music Ltd, London

# 30. Op. 27 No. 11

Robert Volkmann

**Schnell**

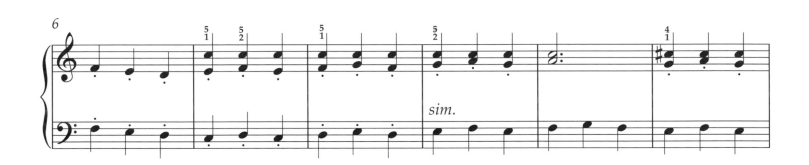

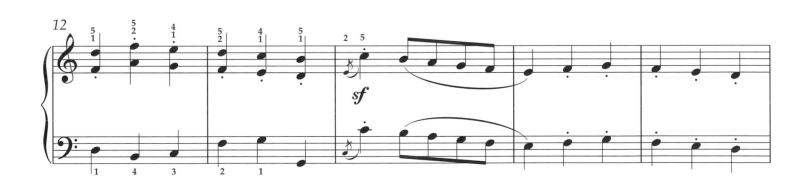

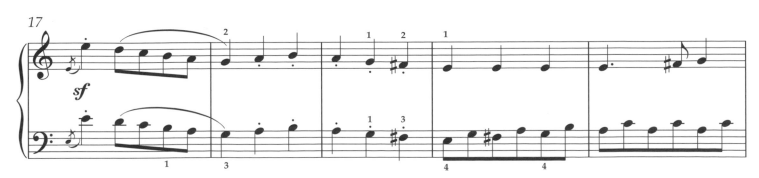

## CD Track List / Plages du CD / CD-Titelverzeichnis

| No. | Title | Composer | Duration |
| --- | --- | --- | --- |
| 1. | Allegretto Grazioso | Cornelius Gurlitt | 0:42 |
| 2. | Mélodie | Félix Le Couppey | 0:36 |
| 3. | Song without Words | Fritz Spindler | 0:37 |
| 4. | Air arabe | Félix Le Couppey | 0:43 |
| 5. | Bärentanz | Robert Schumann | 0:45 |
| 6. | Prelude | Carl Reinecke | 0:35 |
| 7. | Stückchen | Robert Schumann | 0:53 |
| 8. | Gavotte | Cornelius Gurlitt | 0:37 |
| 9. | Petite pièce | Vincent d'Indy | 0:44 |
| 10. | Melodie | Robert Schumann | 0:58 |
| 11. | Soldatenmarsch | Robert Schumann | 0:46 |
| 12. | Arabesque | Johann Burgmüller | 0:59 |
| 13. | Allegro non Troppo | Cornelius Gurlitt | 0:41 |
| 14. | Les Pifferari | Charles Gounod | 0:54 |
| 15. | Stolzer Reitersmann | Robert Fuchs | 0:53 |
| 16. | Étude No. 17 | Félix Le Couppey | 0:41 |
| 17. | Étude No. 15 | Félix Le Couppey | 0:41 |
| 18. | Andante in F Minor | Bedrich Smetana | 0:43 |
| 19. | Through the Desert | Sergei Bortkiewicz | 0:59 |
| 20. | Bourrée | Frédéric Chopin | 0:48 |
| 21. | Haschemann | Robert Schumann | 0:51 |
| 22. | The Doll's Illness | Peter Tchaikovsky | 1:28 |
| 23. | Banges Herzelein | Robert Fuchs | 1:01 |
| 24. | Op. 27 No. 3 | Robert Volkmann | 1:15 |
| 25. | Polka | Mikhail Glinka | 0:26 |
| 26. | Allegretto | Nicolai Rimsky-Korsakov | 0:59 |
| 27. | The New Doll | Peter Tchaikovsky | 0:39 |
| 28. | Invention | Sergey Lyapunov | 0:47 |
| 29. | Kuckuck im Versteck | Robert Schumann | 0:56 |
| 30. | Op. 27 No. 11 | Robert Volkmann | 0:47 |
| | **Total duration** | | **24:24** |

## Schott Editions

BURGMÜLLER, 'Arabesque' – *25 Easy Studies*, op. 100 (Schott Piano Classics; ED 173 © 1985 Schott Musik International, Mainz)

CHOPIN, 'Bourrée' – *3 piano pieces* (Ates Orga; ED 10984 © 1968 Schott Music, London)

GURLITT, 'Gavotte' – *The first Performance*, op. 210 (Edition Schott; ED 196 © 1932 Schott Musik International, Mainz)

LE COUPPEY, 'Air arabe' – *Piano Kids Classic Fun* (Hans-Günter Heumann; ED 8946 © 1999 Schott Musik International, Mainz)

SCHUMANN, 'Bärentanz', 'Stückchen', 'Melodie', 'Soldatenmarsch', 'Haschemann', 'Kuckuck im Versteck' – *Album for the Young* (Schott Piano Classics; ED 9010 © 1997 Schott Musik International, Mainz)

TCHAIKOVSKY, 'The Doll's Illness', 'The New Doll' – *Easy Romantic Piano Music*, vol. 1 (Fritz Emonts; ED 4748 © 1994 and 2002 Schott Musik International, Mainz)